Memoirs Publishing

Author: Suzanne Fortin

Publisher:
MEMOIRS PUBLISHING
96, Boulanger North
Victoriaville, Québec
Canada
G6T 1B1

Tel.: (819) 751-3060
Fax: (819) 751-5188
Toll free: 1-888-963-6647
E-mail: memoires@ivic.qc.ca

Graphic Design and Layout: CONSTANCE DESSIN PRO
Printer: HÉON & NADEAU LIMITED, VICTORIAVILLE

English adaptation: LONG & ASSOCIATES

ISBN 0-9684627-1-5

Dear friend,

Thank you for purchasing The World's Best Story...Your Own. This personalized questionnaire will provide untold enjoyment as you reminisce and set to writing those wonderful moments from your earliest childhood onwards which otherwise would be lost in the mists of time.

From the richness of your memories will emerge your own, unique written story. The joy of your recollections will heighten as you share them with family and close ones. And, as a legacy standing the test of time, their value for future generations will be immense.

Sincerely yours,
Suzanne Fortin

SUMMARY

Introduction.. 4

Suggestions.. 6

Reminders.. 7

Recollections of : photo.................................... 12

Your parents.. 13

Your birth.. 19

Your relatives.. 23

Your childhood.. 28

Your childhood Christmases.................................... 36

School.. 39

At home... 44

Photos.. 52

Your teenage years.. 53

Your marriage... 70

Your children... 79

Your work... 96

Your life now... 107

What you may wish to add...................................... 117

CHARTS

Ancestors... 17

Other known ancestors..................................... 18

Brothers and sisters.. 21

Maternal aunts and uncles................................. 24

Paternal aunts and uncles.................................. 26

Primary schools.. 43

High schools, colleges and universities..................... 60

Your addresses... 77

Your children.. 83

Employment.. 97

Your spouse's employment.................................. 99

INTRODUCTION

Skim through the questionnaire to get used to the subject matter and relevant questions. Jot down facts simply, but as detailed as possible, as you recall them. Think of what you would have wanted to know about your parents or grandparents and relate your own souvenirs.

Looking at old photos will help revive moments of the past. Listening to music of yesteryear can also assist your recollecting.

Answer as many questions as possible. If some facts and dates have been forgotten, mark the appropriate sections with a question mark (?). By leaving these aside, you will be surprised by what you remember after a few days or weeks.

Reminiscence quickly becomes an on-going process. In completing the questionnaire, one souvenir will prompt another. Make a quick note of the latter for reference as the proper response to a further question. If you require more

4

space than that allotted for your answers, use the lined pages at the end of the questionnaire or simply add more pages.

Most importantly, just take your time. Enjoy these golden moments of your recollections and, once completed, share in the happiness of family and close ones who will benefit from a truly wonderful legacy, your very own life story!

HAPPY MEMORIES ! MEMOIRS PUBLISHING

SUGGESTIONS

*   Always keep a notepad and pencil handy. A souvenir may pop up at any time…

*   You may want to draft your answers on paper prior to transcribing them in your book.

*   If you prefer not to write, you could record your answers on an audio tape machine. You could then ask someone whom you know to write for you. You could also involve one of your children or grandchildren who, while writing, would enjoy your happy recollecting.

*   You can include photos in your book; photos of your parents, you as a child, teenager, young adult, your house, your children and grandchildren, etc… Fix them to 8 ½ by 11 inch sheets of paper and get laser photocopies made. (The result is fabulous.) You can increase or decrease their size as needed. Then, simply glue the laser photos on the appropriate white photos pages in your book.

*   Do not worry about the quality or style of your writing. The aim of this book is not one of literary awards but rather to recollect facts which will relate your life to others. When the story of a loved one is told, simple straightforward content precludes style.

*   Make use of the questionnaire's reminder sections (objects of the past, places, persons, etc.) which will rekindle your memories.

REMINDERS
OBJECTS

- butter churn ✓
- wool spinning wheel
- sewing machine ✓
- roller-style clothes washer ✓
- scrubbing board ✓
- harsh soap
- linen iron
- curling iron
- hairpiece
- make-up
- oil lamp ✓
- wood stove ✓
- well ✓
- food icebox ✓
- homemade preserves ✓
- water pump
- grandfather clock
- trophy
- frame
- crucifix
- statue
- scapular
- rosary
- medal

- diploma ✓
- report card ✓
- strap
- small whip
- swing/seesaw ✓
- hammock ✓
- piano ✓
- accordion ✓
- harmonica ✓
- violin ✓
- guitar ✓
- drum
- juke-box
- musical box
- gramophone ✓
- radio ✓ license
- black and white ✓
- television ✓
- color television ✓
- telephone ✓
- newspapers ✓
- mousetrap
- chimney ✓

REMINDERS
PLACES

- summer kitchen
- general store √
- church/synagogue
- post office √
- inn
- bank
- dance hall √
- restaurant
- barn
- cow shed
- forest
- lake
- river/stream √
- library
- garden √
- attic
- basement
- cellar √
- shed
- convent
- college

- cottage
- arena
- playground
- summer camp
- skating rink √
- seashore
- presbytery
- sugar shack

REMINDERS
PERSONS

- doctor
- notary/lawyer
- parish priest/rabbi
- photographer
- midwife
- nurse
- nun
- policeman
- baker
- milkman
- postman
- blacksmith
- mayor
- lumberjack
- baby-sitter
- Santa Claus
- werewolf
- witch

- elf
- fairy
- ghost
- clairvoyant
- fortuneteller
- hippies
- hero
- pirate
- Indian
- soldier

REMINDERS
GAMES

- blindman's buff ✓
- spin-the-bottle ✓
- tag ✓
- football
- monopoly
- cards ✓
- poker
- bingo
- kite
- canoe
- raft ✓
- ice skates ✓
- roller skates ✓
- snowshoes
- snow-bike
- motorcycle
- bow
- rifle
- hockey
- baseball
- hunting
- fishing

- camping
- snow sleigh ✓
- merry-go-round
- running
- tennis
- soccer
- swimming ✓

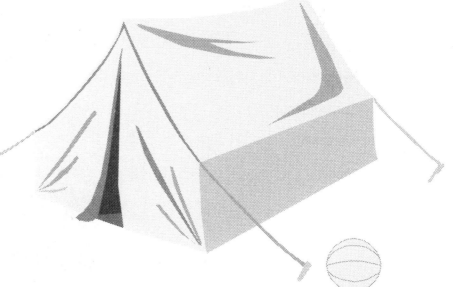

REMINDERS

OTHERS

- scouts
- girl guides
- majorettes
- brass band
- army
- parade
- punishment
- inheritance
- fire
- flood
- picnic ✓
- hurricane
- snowstorm ✓
- eclipse
- rainbow
- parish visit
- miracle
- magic
- fair
- astrology
- caroling ✓

- fairy-tale
- hay-making ✓
- hitch-hiking ✓
- funerals ✓
- divorce ✓
- fine
- flying saucer
- tornado

THE RECOLLECTIONS OF

*Photo taken at age:*_____

YOUR PARENTS

What do you know about your parents' childhood?

Your mother's?

_____

_____

_____

_____

Your father's?

_____

_____

_____

_____

How did your parents meet?

_____

_____

_____

_____

How long did they go out with each other?

_____

_____

_____

_____

When and where did they wed?

_____

_____

How old were they when married?

_____

_____

Anecdotes on their wedding or honeymoon.

_____

_____

_____

_____

_____

_____

Did your parents come from large families?

Mother :   How many brothers?   _____1_____

                How many sisters?   _____0_____

Was she the eldest, youngest or?   _____eldest_____

Father: How many brothers?   _____0_____

                How many sisters?   _____1_____

Was he the eldest, youngest or?   _____eldest_____

Were their families financially well-off or not?

Your mother: _____

                _____

                _____

                _____

                _____

Your father: _____

                _____

                _____

                _____

                _____

Describe your mother; her personality, appearance, interests, hobbies, philosophy on life, education, trade or profession, etc…

_____

_____

_____

_____

_____

_____

_____

Describe your father; his personality, appearance, interests, hobbies, philosophy on life, education, trade or profession, etc…

_____

_____

_____

_____

_____

_____

ANCESTORS

ANCESTORS	NAME/SURNAME	DATE AND PLACE OF BIRTH	TRADE/ PROFESSION	DATE DECEASED
Maternal grandmother				
Maternal grandfather				
Paternal grandmother				
Paternal grandfather				
Your mother				
Your father				

OTHER KNOWN ANCESTORS

ANCESTORS	NAME/SURNAME	DATE AND PLACE OF BIRTH	TRADE/ PROFESSION	DATE DECEASED
Maternal great grandmother				
Maternal great grandfather				
Paternal great grandmother				
Paternal great grandfather				

YOUR BIRTH

Date of birth:_____ Time:_____

Weight: _____ Height:_____

Where were you born? (city, town, country)_____

_____

Were you born at the hospital or at home?_____

_____

Whom was the doctor or mid-wife assisting your mother during your birth?

_____

_____

Was it an easy delivery?_____

_____

_____

What was your father doing during childbirth?

_____

_____

_____

How old was your mother when you were born?_____

How old was your father when you were born?_____

Are you the eldest, youngest or the_____th (your rank) in a family

of_____children.

How many boys? _____

How many girls? _____

Who chose your name and why were you given that name?

_____

_____

_____

_____

Did your mother breast-feed you?

_____

_____

Who helped your mother after childbirth?

_____

_____

_____

_____

BROTHERS AND SISTERS

NAME	DATE OF BIRTH	MARRIED SPOUSE	NUMBER OF CHILDREN/NAME	DATE DECEASED

BROTHERS AND SISTERS

(Continued...)

NAME	DATE OF BIRTH	MARRIED SPOUSE	NUMBER OF CHILDREN/NAME	DATE DECEASED

RELATIVES

Did you get to know your grandparents? If so, what do you recall about them? Did they influence your life?

_____

_____

_____

_____

_____

Do you remember some aunts or uncles in particular, what role did they play in your life?

_____

_____

_____

_____

What are your recollections of cousins, nephews and nieces?

_____

_____

_____

AUNTS AND UNCLES

On your **mother's** side, list her brothers and sisters, including herself, in the order of the eldest to the youngest.

NAME	TRADE/ PROFESSION	MARRIED SPOUSE	NUMBER OF CHILDREN/NAME	DATE DECEASED

AUNTS AND UNCLES

(Continued...)

On your **mother's** side.

NAME	TRADE/ PROFESSION	MARRIED SPOUSE	NUMBER OF CHILDREN/NAME	DATE DECEASED

AUNTS AND UNCLES

On your **father's** side, list his brothers and sisters, including himself, in the order of the eldest to the youngest.

NAME	TRADE/ PROFESSION	MARRIED SPOUSE	NUMBER OF CHILDREN/NAME	DATE DECEASED

AUNTS AND UNCLES

(continued...)

On your **father's** side.

NAME	TRADE/ PROFESSION	MARRIED SPOUSE	NUMBER OF CHILDREN/NAME	DATE DECEASED

YOUR CHILDHOOD

What was the address of your first home?

_____

_____

Describe the house in which you grew up (its exterior and interior, the
number of rooms, the wall coloring, the furniture, etc.).

_____

_____

_____

_____

_____

_____

How was your bedroom? Did you share it with sisters or brothers?

_____

_____

_____

_____

_____

Can you describe the city or town where you were raised?

_____

_____

_____

_____

_____

Who were your neighbors? Did you visit often?

_____

_____

_____

_____

_____

Did your parents move often when you were a child? Do you remember the addresses?

_____

_____

_____

_____

What is your earliest memory?

_____

_____

_____

_____

_____

_____

What was your favorite toy?

My tebbybear, sruffy.

_____

_____

_____

What games did you play after school, during the evenings and weekends?

_____

_____

_____

_____

_____

How did you spend your summer holidays?

_____

_____

_____

_____

_____

Did you go swimming, where and with who?

_____

_____

_____

What games did you play during winter?

sleding

Who did you play with? (friends, neighbors, brothers, sisters)
Whom was your best friend?

I play with my brother, and my brother is my best friend

How did you get along with your brothers and sisters?

Very well.

Do you remember the clothes you wore then? Did your mother make them?

Did you have any pets at home? What was the name of one of your cats or dogs?

_____

_____

_____

_____

_____

Did you collect anything? What? How long did you keep your collection?

_____

_____

_____

_____

Did you go on a trip as a child? Where did you go and with who?

_____

_____

_____

_____

_____

_____

Did you have access to a cottage?

_____

_____

_____

_____

Describe your appearance as a child.

_____

_____

_____

Did your father, mother or someone else tell you things you did as a child?

_____

_____

_____

_____

_____

_____

Did you experience any misadventures as a child?

_____

_____

_____

_____

_____

Were you ever very frightened as a child?

_____

_____

_____

_____

As a child, did you ever scare someone?

_____

_____

_____

_____

YOUR CHILDHOOD CHRISTMASES

How was Christmas or the Holiday Season in your home?

_____

_____

_____

_____

_____

_____

_____

_____

_____

Did you believe in Santa Claus? Until what age?

_____

_____

_____

_____

_____

What kind of gifts did you receive?

_____

_____

_____

_____

Which was the most beautiful gift you received; from who?

_____

_____

_____

_____

_____

Did you offer gifts as well?

_____

_____

_____

_____

_____

Was there a Christmas tree? Who decorated it and in what fashion?

_____

_____

_____

_____

How was New Year's at your house?

_____

_____

_____

_____

_____

_____

Did you father bless the family?

_____

_____

_____

Do you remember your very first day of school? Were you eager to go? Who brought you and how were you dressed?

_____

_____

_____

_____

What kind of school was yours? Were boys and girls mixed in the same classroom?

_____

_____

Do you remember your first teacher?

_____

_____

_____

Did you like school?

_____

_____

_____

What kind of student were you?

_____

_____

_____

_____

_____

What was your preferred subject matter? Which did you like the least?

_____

_____

_____

_____

Did you have lunch at school or at home?

_____

_____

_____

How did you get to school, by bus, bicycle or foot?

_____

_____

_____

_____

Do you remember your First Communion or other first important religious ceremony?

_____

_____

_____

_____

_____

In which church or synagogue was the ceremony held? How were you dressed, etc.?

_____

_____

_____

Who were your godfather and godmother?

_____

_____

_____

Did they offer you gifts? On what occasion?

_____

_____

_____

_____

Do you recall your first religious confessions? What did you think about sin?

_____

_____

_____

_____

_____

_____

_____

Did you miss school ? Why?

_____

_____

_____

_____

_____

_____

_____

PRIMARY SCHOOL

SCHOOL/ADDRESS	DEGREE YEAR	TEACHER	GOOD FRIENDS

AT HOME

What were your chores at home?

_____

_____

_____

_____

What kind of child were you?

_____

_____

_____

Were your parents strict? Give some examples.

_____

_____

_____

Did they use favored words or expressions?

_____

_____

Were they superstitious?

_____

_____

_____

_____

How important was religion? Did you attend religious services frequently with your family?

_____

_____

_____

_____

_____

_____

_____

Were you afraid of Hell?

_____

_____

_____

_____

Do you remember Easter or Passover as a child?

_____

_____

_____

_____

_____

_____

How were birthdays celebrated?

_____

_____

_____

_____

_____

Did you dress up for Halloween?

_____

_____

_____

_____

_____

Did your mother hum songs or tell you stories? Which ones?

_____

_____

_____

_____

How were the meals your mother prepared? What was your favorite dish?

_____

_____

_____

_____

Did you ever get mad as a child?

_____

_____

_____

_____

What was your nickname and who used it?

_____

_____

_____

Did you have a piggy bank? Who gave you money and what use did you make of it?

_____

_____

_____

_____

_____

Were there musicians or other talents in your family?

_____

_____

_____

_____

_____

Did you, your brothers or sisters or your parents have an accident?

_____

_____

_____

_____

_____

As a child, were you sick and/or hospitalized? (Measles, chickenpox or mumps for example?)

_____

_____

_____

_____

Did a family member or close one die during your childhood? How did you react?

_____

_____

_____

_____

Do you recall your father's cars and the transportation means of the day?

_____

_____

_____

Which person influenced your childhood? In what manner?

_____

_____

_____

_____

Which event marked your childhood?

_____

_____

_____

_____

What was your greatest joy as a child?

_____

_____

_____

_____

And which was your greatest sorrow?

_____

_____

_____

_____

When did your parents purchase a television set and which show did you watch?

_____

_____

What was the fashion of the times? Which clothes, music, games?

_____

_____

_____

_____

Did you sometimes cry?

_____

_____

_____

_____

Was your childhood a happy one?

_____

_____

_____

_____

_____

_____

PHOTOS

YOUR TEENAGE YEARS

Were you a quiet or mischievous teenager? Describe your personality and physical aspect during those years.

_____

_____

_____

_____

_____

Where did you live? Describe your bedroom, the house and the neighborhood.

_____

_____

_____

_____

What were your hobbies or leisure activities?

_____

_____

_____

Were you fond of sports?

_____

_____

_____

_____

Were you sick, victim of an accident or hospitalized?

_____

_____

_____

_____

Whom was your best friend and what did you do together?

_____

_____

_____

_____

Were you part of a gang? If so, what were the group's activities?

_____

_____

_____

How did you get along with your brothers and sisters?

_____

_____

_____

_____

Did you get along well with your parents or were they subjected to your
"adolescent crisis"?

_____

_____

_____

_____

Were you closer to your mother or your father?

_____

_____

_____

_____

How was the relationship between your parents?

_____

_____

_____

_____

Do you remember your first bicycle?

_____

_____

_____

_____

Were there fairs, exhibitions and amusement parks?

_____

_____

_____

Did you go to the theater? Which movies did you like?

_____

_____

_____

_____

What did you watch on television?

_____

_____

_____

_____

_____

Do you recall when you received electricity, the telephone?

_____

_____

_____

_____

How was shopping in those days?

_____

_____

_____

_____

Did you have a record player and what music did you prefer listening?

_____

_____

_____

Did you like reading? What did you read?

_____

_____

_____

_____

Did you play pranks on your friends or did they do so on you?

_____

_____

_____

_____

Which high school did you attend?

_____

_____

What did you do after school, in the evenings and on weekends?

_____

_____

_____

_____

_____

How did you spend your summer holidays?

_____

_____

_____

_____

Did you smoke? With your parents' consent?

_____

_____

_____

_____

_____

Were politics discussed at home?

_____

_____

_____

_____

How was your schooling? What level did you reach? When did you stop and why?

_____

_____

_____

_____

_____

_____

HIGH SHOOL, COLLEGE AND UNIVERSITY

SCHOOL/ADDRESS	DEGREE YEAR	TEACHER PROFESSOR	GOOD FRIENDS

60

As a youth, did you have to work?

_____

_____

_____

_____

What was your first job? How long did you hold it?

_____

_____

_____

What did you do with your first wages? How much did you earn then?

_____

_____

_____

Did you have to remit some money to your parents?

_____

_____

_____

Did war affect your life? Can you recall souvenirs of the first or second world war?

_____

_____

_____

_____

Is there an event which marked your teenage years?

_____

_____

_____

_____

_____

_____

Which person influenced your adolescence?

_____

_____

_____

_____

_____

Were you ever heartbroken as a teenager?

_____

_____

_____

_____

_____

Relate a great joy as a teenager.

_____

_____

_____

_____

_____

_____

Relate a great sorrow as a teenager.

_____

_____

_____

_____

_____

_____

Were alcoholic beverages served in your family? When did you have your first drink?

_____

_____

_____

_____

_____

_____

Do you remember being mad as a teenager?

_____

_____

_____

_____

_____

When did you obtain your driving license? Who taught you to drive?

_____

_____

_____

_____

_____

Recount your first kiss.

_____

_____

_____

_____

Describe your first boyfriend or girlfriend.

_____

_____

_____

_____

_____

Describe the others, if any.

_____

_____

_____

_____

_____

_____

Was sexuality a taboo? What sex education did you receive?

_____

_____

_____

_____

_____

How did you meet your spouse?

_____

_____

_____

_____

How old were you both?

_____

Relate your going out period.

_____

_____

_____

_____

_____

What did you talk about together? Was a "chaperon" present?

_____

_____

_____

_____

Where were you the first time you kissed?

_____

_____

_____

_____

Did you dance? Where and with what kind of music?

_____

_____

_____

_____

How did the request for marriage occur? Where? Whom proposed?

_____

_____

_____

_____

How long had you been going out together?

_____

_____

(Woman) Did your boyfriend ask your father for your hand in marriage? Recount what happened.

(Man) Did you ask your girlfriend's father for her hand in marriage? Recount what happened.

_____

_____

_____

_____

_____

_____

_____

_____

Did you get engaged? Where and when?

_____

_____

_____

Did you follow a marriage preparation course?

_____

_____

_____

_____

IF YOUR HAVE BEEN MARRIED MORE THAN ONCE

SPOUSE   DATE OF MARRIAGE

_____   _____

_____   _____

_____   _____

If you are single or unmarried, explain why and enumerate the advantages and inconveniences.

_____

_____

_____

_____

_____

YOUR MARRIAGE

What is the date of your marriage?_____

In which church or synagogue was the ceremony held? What is the name of the priest or rabbi who celebrated your marriage?

_____

_____

_____

Did you have bridesmaids, best men and a flower girl?

_____

_____

_____

_____

How old were both of you?

_____

Which car did you use for the occasion? Who was the chauffeur?

_____

_____

_____

Were you nervous the prior evening and the day of your wedding?

_____

_____

_____

_____

How was the bride's gown? Was it bought or made by a close one?

_____

_____

_____

_____

How was the groom attired?

_____

_____

_____

Where was the reception held?

_____

_____

Were there many guests?

_____

_____

_____

Do you remember the menu?

_____

_____

_____

_____

Which orchestra played and on what song did you first dance as newlyweds?

_____

_____

_____

_____

List a few gifts you received.

_____

_____

_____

_____

_____

Did you have a honeymoon? Where did you go and for how long? If not, why did you not have a honeymoon?

_____

_____

_____

_____

_____

_____

_____

_____

Do you want to relate your wedding night?

_____

_____

_____

_____

_____

_____

_____

Describe your spouse then (personality, appearance, hobbies, qualities, faults, occupation, etc.).

_____

_____

_____

_____

_____

_____

_____

How did you get along with your in-laws? Describe them.

_____

_____

_____

_____

_____

_____

_____

How did your spouse get along with your family?

_____

_____

_____

_____

_____

_____

Once married, where did you live?

_____

_____

_____

_____

Describe your first house.

_____

_____

_____

_____

_____

Did you move often? For what reasons? Do you remember the addresses of the homes you lived in? Inscribe them on the following page.

_____

_____

_____

_____

_____

_____

_____

Describe your first car.

_____

_____

_____

_____

_____

_____

_____

ADDRESSES

List your addresses from your birth until now.

NUMBER, STREET, TOWN	FOR HOW LONG ?	TENANT OR OWNER	WITH WHO DID YOU LIVE ?

ADDRESSES

(continued...)

List your addresses from your birth until now.

NUMBER, STREET, TOWN	FOR HOW LONG ?	TENANT OR OWNER	WITH WHO DID YOU LIVE ?

YOUR CHILDREN

How many children did you have? _____

How old were you at the birth of your first child?

You: _____   Your spouse: _____

(Woman) How did you feel when pregnant?
(Man)   How did your wife feel when she was pregnant?

_____

_____

_____

_____

Where were your children born? At home or the hospital?

_____

_____

_____

(Woman) Who assisted you during childbirth?
(Man)   Who assisted your wife during childbirth?

_____

_____

_____

(Woman) What did your husband do during childbirth?
(Man) What did you do during childbirth?

_____

_____

_____

Who chose your children's names?

_____

_____

_____

Did some of your children die at birth or at a young age?

_____

_____

_____

Relate the baptism or first religious rite of your children.

_____

_____

_____

_____

_____

Were your children breast-fed?

_____

_____

_____

_____

_____

How did you rate yourself as a parent? Strict, permissive, over-nurturing?

YOU: _____

_____

_____

_____

_____

_____

YOUR SPOUSE:_____

_____

_____

_____

_____

_____

Who took care of your children's education?

_____

_____

_____

_____

_____

Were your children quiet or mischievous?

_____

_____

_____

_____

_____

_____

Did brothers and sisters get along?

_____

_____

_____

_____

YOUR CHILDREN

NAME	DATE OF BIRTH	MARRIED SPOUSE	NUMBER OF CHILDREN/NAME	TRADE/ PROFESSION

YOUR CHILDREN

(continued...)

NAME	DATE OF BIRTH	MARRIED SPOUSE	NUMBER OF CHILDREN/NAME	TRADE/ PROFESSION

Recount some anecdotes which best describe your children. Relate some qualities and faults of each of them.

_____

_____

_____

_____

_____

_____

_____

_____

_____

_____

_____

_____

_____

_____

Did your children like school? What kind of students do you think they were?

_____

_____

_____

_____

_____

Did you play pranks on your children and did they do so on you? On April's Fools Day, for example.

_____

_____

_____

_____

_____

Did you have family outings? Where did you go with the children?

_____

_____

_____

_____

_____

At home, what family activities did you do?

_____

_____

_____

_____

_____

_____

Were your children sick or victims of accidents?

_____

_____

_____

_____

_____

Did you or your spouse get sick during those years?

_____

_____

_____

_____

_____

What were your children's chores at home?

_____

_____

_____

_____

_____

_____

_____

_____

What did they do after school?

_____

_____

_____

_____

_____

_____

_____

_____

How did they spend their summer holidays?

_____

_____

_____

_____

_____

Did you have a cottage?

_____

_____

_____

_____

Did you have pets at home?

_____

_____

_____

_____

_____

How was life then?

_____

_____

_____

_____

_____

_____

_____

_____

_____

What was in fashion? Did your children follow fashion trends?

_____

_____

_____

_____

_____

Was there ever any alcohol or drug-related problems?

_____

_____

_____

_____

_____

_____

_____

What were the responsibilities of your spouse and yourself at home? Were respective roles well-defined?

_____

_____

_____

_____

_____

_____

_____

_____

Did you travel?

_____

_____

_____

_____

Do you speak another language? Where and how did you learn it?

_____

_____

_____

_____

How was Christmas or the Holiday Season? What about the New Year? Did your children believe in Santa Claus?

_____

_____

_____

_____

_____

_____

How did you celebrate Easter or Passover with your children?

_____

_____

_____

_____

Did you spoil your children?

_____

_____

_____

_____

_____

Are there principles you wanted to transmit to them and do you believe you
have succeeded?

_____

_____

_____

_____

_____

_____

What were your leisure activities and those of your spouse while you raised your family?

_____

_____

_____

_____

_____

_____

_____

_____

Was religion important for your family?

_____

_____

_____

_____

_____

_____

_____

As a parent, what is your best recollection?

_____

_____

_____

_____

_____

_____

_____

And which one is the worst?

_____

_____

_____

_____

_____

_____

_____

How many jobs have you held? Which one was the best and which one the worst? Why? List the others on the following page.

Did your spouse hold many jobs?

_____

_____

_____

_____

_____

_____

_____

JOBS

EMPLOYER	POSITION TITLE	DATE FROM___ TO ___	SALARY $	REASON FOR LEAVING /COMMENTS

JOBS

(continued...)

EMPLOYER	POSITION TITLE	DATE FROM___ TO ___	SALARY $	REASON FOR LEAVING /COMMENTS

YOUR SPOUSE'S JOBS

EMPLOYER	POSITION TITLE	DATE FROM___ TO ___	SALARY $	REASON FOR LEAVING /COMMENTS

(continued...)

EMPLOYER	POSITION TITLE	DATE FROM___ TO ___	SALARY $	REASON FOR LEAVING /COMMENTS

In which occupational field did you wish to work as a younger person? Were you employed in this area? If not, why did you pursue another trade or profession?

_____

_____

_____

_____

_____

_____

_____

Did you or your spouse ever receive unemployment insurance allowances or other social security benefits? Explain the circumstances.

_____

_____

_____

_____

_____

_____

_____

Who was your best boss and why?

_____

_____

_____

_____

_____

Did you do any volunteer work?

_____

_____

_____

_____

Did you take courses?

_____

_____

_____

_____

How did you feel when your children left home to get married or pursue their lives elsewhere?

_____

_____

_____

_____

_____

Did you or your spouse offer advice to your children as they got married? What advice?

_____

_____

_____

_____

How did you react the first time you became grandparents? How old were you then?

_____

_____

_____

_____

Do you have grandchildren and great grandchildren? Name them.

_____

_____

_____

_____

_____

_____

Are your parents still living and, if so, what do they do? If not, when did they pass away, of what cause and how did you react?

_____

_____

_____

_____

_____

_____

_____

_____

_____

Are you widowed? Since when? Relate.

_____

_____

_____

_____

_____

_____

_____

Are you currently retired or when will you be?

_____

_____

_____

_____

_____

_____

_____

_____

What will you do when retired? Are you worried about retirement?

_____

_____

_____

_____

_____

_____

_____

What are the differences between your life as a child and teenager and life now?

_____

_____

_____

_____

_____

_____

_____

YOUR LIFE NOW

Where do you presently reside? Since when?

_____

_____

_____

_____

What are your current leisure activities?

_____

_____

_____

_____

Who are your friends and what do you do together?

_____

_____

_____

_____

_____

_____

What kind of music do you like? Who are your preferred singers?

_____

_____

_____

What do you like to watch on television?

_____

_____

_____

_____

Do you like reading? What type of books do you read?

_____

_____

_____

What kind of movies do you like? Who are your favorite actors?

_____

_____

_____

_____

Which country would you want to visit? Why?

_____

_____

_____

_____

What is the best advice you received?

_____

_____

_____

_____

_____

Which persons or events most marked your life?

_____

_____

_____

_____

_____

How do you find life today? (Drugs, AIDS, etc...)

_____

_____

_____

_____

_____

_____

_____

What do you think about life after life? Does death scare you?

_____

_____

_____

_____

_____

_____

_____

_____

Do you have any projects?

_____

_____

_____

_____

What makes you happy?

_____

_____

_____

_____

Does something make you sad?

_____

_____

_____

_____

What would you want people to say of you?

_____

_____

_____

_____

Which achievement are you the proudest of?

_____

_____

_____

_____

_____

_____

_____

Are you healthy and what do you do to stay so? If not, which illnesses or worries afflict your health?

_____

_____

_____

_____

_____

_____

What advice would you give your children now?

_____

_____

_____

_____

_____

_____

_____

What would you change if you redid your life?

_____

_____

_____

_____

_____

_____

Why are you writing your life's story? How old are you now?

_____

_____

_____

_____

_____

_____

How would you entitle your story? Why?

_____

_____

_____

What is your philosophy on life?

_____

_____

_____

_____

_____

Have you things to say to your children who will read your story?

_____

_____

_____

_____

_____

_____

_____

Is there a poem or phrase you may wish to add?

_____

_____

_____

_____

_____

_____

How was the experience of relating your life story by writing your memoirs?

_____

_____

_____

_____

_____

_____

Are you eager to share your story with close ones?

_____

_____

_____

_____

Would you recommend others write their life story? Why?

_____

_____

_____

_____

What you may wish to add.

_____

_____

_____

_____

_____

_____

_____

_____

_____

_____

_____

_____

_____

_____

_____

_____

SERVICES OFFERED

RETRANSCRIPTION OF YOUR MANUSCRIPT

Once the questionnaire is completed, you may keep it as is or make a book of it. To do so, you need only call *Memoirs Publishing*. Our seasoned editorial staff and other professionals will transform the recollections and facts in your questionnaire into your very own beautifully-printed, bond book.

OUR BOOK FORMATS

Standard Edition
* Hard cover
* Durable German-type glued binding
* Printed on premium-quality paper
* Format: 5 ½ inches wide by 8 ½ inches high
* Photos in black and white

Deluxe Edition
* Hard cover with gold printing
* Durable German-type glued binding
* Printed on premium-quality paper
* Format: 5 ½ inches wide by 8 ½ inches high
* Photos in color and/or black and white
* Elegant, protective bookcase

For more information, please contact:

MEMOIRS PUBLISHING
96, Boulanger North
Victoriaville, Québec
Canada
G6T 1B1
Tel.: (819) 751-3060
Fax: (819) 751-5188
Toll Free: **1-888-963-6647**
E-mail: memoires@ivic.qc.ca